Betrayal In Your Beekman Arms

Poetry

by Joan Noëldechen

ISBN: 978-1-257-56788-1

LULU.COM

FOR JEHOVAH,
OUR FATHER SEES ALL

THAW

THE SNOW MELTS

OVER TIME

AND I KNOW

SPRING LIES

UNDERNEATH

THE FROZEN

CRYSTALS

WAITING TO

MELT AWAY

BEFORE THE GLORY OF THE SUN.

UNICORN

MAGIC HORSES

RIDE AWAY

FROM NEW HOPE

NOT FEARFUL

OF ANOTHER DAY

WHEN HORSES

WEEP IN THE

CORRAL.

THE WARREN

SAFE

IN THE GROUND

I PEER INTO

THE SKY AND I FEEL FREE

TO SOAR

IN MY

MIND'S EYE,

DANCING

ABOVE THE CLOUDS.

ANTHONY

ARTIST

TENDING TO THE BARFLIES,

HIDING TATTOOS BENEATH

A STARCHED WHITE

CRISPNESS.

HE MAY STILL LEAP TO THE FRONT

AND JAM UNTIL DAWN.

LARRY'S HOME

LIVING

IN HEAVEN

WITH WIFELY BLISS,

DREAMING OF

DEAD GOATS,

SPILLING, OVERFLOWING

PROPHECY

IN SYMBOLIC

PRECISION

IN ORDER TO FIND

FULL LAWNS TO HARVEST.

CHEWING ON

GREENERY KEEPS

THEM WHOLE AND HAPPY.

LAUREN

KEEPER OF THE DRINK

AND PEPPER

TUCKED BEHIND

AN ARRAY OF BRIGHT,

CLEAR WINE GLASSES.

SHE TURNS ON

A SPIN

LIKE A BRIGHT MERCURY DIME.

THE MAGIC

IS HERE FOR THE MOMENT

AS SHE LAYS DOWN

THE COASTERS

AND FREE COUNCIL.

STARKNESS

CRADLE MY LOVE

IN A SAFER PLACE.

ONCE I FIND THE TRUTH

ABOUT MYSELF,

I MAY JOIN HIM

IN A DEEP

SLEEP OF

CONTENTMENT AND PEACE.

THE SAGE

A WOMAN

COMES OUT

OF THE DESERT

WITH WORDS

OF WISDOM

WHICH

SEARS MY SOUL

TO MY CONSCIOUS THOUGHTS AND MAKES

A UNIQUE

DESIGN UPON

MY LIFE

AND IN THE LIVES OF OTHERS.

THE BEEKMAN

THE ROAD IS THE SAME.

THE PASSENGERS STOP

TO DRINK AND DINE.

THE WOMEN SMILE SEDUCTIVELY

BEFORE THEIR

LIPS TOUCH

THE GLASS

AND THE MEN

SPEAK OF BUSINESS DEALS

AND DREAMS

IN REAL TIME.

KID

I DO NOT SEE YOU,

BUT YOU ARE IN

MY HEART

NO MATTER WHERE

YOU ARE OR

WHO YOU'RE WITH.

AMBER

LITTLE, STRONG, SMART,

AND QUICK,

WORKER OF THE ROOM

PILES DISHES

HIGH UPON THE TABLE

FOR THE PATRONS

TO SAMPLE.

CHOCOLATE CAKE AND STRAWBERRY TARTS

ABOVE THE TRAY.

I HANG OUT

JUST TO WATCH THE MIRACLE OF HER INDUSTRY

AND JOY.

A TOAST

MAY YOU FIND

THE BLESSINGS

IN EACH

MOMENT OF YOUR DAY,

EVEN IF YOU ARE NOT LOOKING FOR THEM.

TEA

A PORCELAIN WHITE POT

WARMS ME WITH

ITS TOUCH.

THE BAG IS STEEPING

AS I PONDER

THE CHOICE OF LEMON

VERSUS MILK.

THE DANCE

A TAKEN MAN ASKED ME

WHY I WASN'T MARRIED

OR WITH SOMEONE AND I ANSWERED,

"I USED TO BE."

HE SAID, "I DON'T UNDERSTAND WHY YOU ARE NOT TAKEN NOW."

I SAID, "IT'S NOT MEANT FOR ME, BUT I'M GLAD TO SEE YOU WITH SOMEONE SO LOVELY. IT MAKES ME HAPPY TO SEE COUPLES LIKE YOURSELVES."

THEY SMILED AS THEY LEFT

ME SITTING AT MIDNIGHT,

CURLING UP WITH A TIMES.

THE IGNORANT ENEMY

YOU ARE FILLED

WITH NOTHINGNESS

AND AN INWARD CHILDISH HOLLOWNESS

I ASK GOD TO BLESS YOU AND FORGIVE YOU

EVERY NIGHT

I ASK GOD FOR FORGIVENESS FOR FAILING TO MAKE THE PEACE BETWEEN US.

YOU HATE ME,

BUT I SHAN'T ASK WHY.

THE HATRED LIES

IN YOUR HEART,

NOT MINE.

I ASKED GOD

TO DECIDE

YOUR FATE.

I AM NOT YOUR JUDGE,

NOR JURY.

MY LIFE

MEANS LITTLE

TO YOU

AS YOU'VE SHOWN ME.

TIME AND AGAIN

I HAVE PITIED

YOUR IGNORANCE.

YOU HAVE ONLY HURT

YOURSELF IN

ATTEMPTING

TO HURT ME.

THE IRISH WAVE

I SAW YOUR FACE AND

READ SORROW AS YOU MISSED

THE LOVE OF YOUR LIFE.

DEATH WAS ALL AROUND YOU STILL AND I, NO ONE,

WISHED FOR GOD

TO REMOVE THE STING

FROM YOUR HEART.

GOD BLESS YOU.

DO NOT FEAR.

I HAD MY REASONS FOR

DROPPING FLOWERS

AND A LADY'S PORTRAIT

UPON YOUR TRUE LOVE'S GRAVE.

THE FORMER PARK

THERE IS NO PARK

WITH DUCKS

AND SWANS.

NO CHILDREN LAUGHING

WITH THEIR BEAUTIFUL MOTHERS.

JUST A CONSTRUCTION VEHICLE

ABOVE A DIRT ABYSS.

LET'S SAY A PRAYER FOR HEALING,

SO ALL MAY RETURN

BY SUMMER'S LIGHT.

THE LAST SUPPER

CUT , BRUISED

AND IN SHOCK

AS YOU SWARMED

MY SOCIAL PLACE,

I LEFT VOWING TO NEVER RETURN.

WHO WOULD WANT TO BE

IN THE COMPANY

OF DRUNKEN FOOLS

AND HARDENED HEARTS.

YOU TRIED TO KILL ME WITH

YOUR CANCER, BUT I PITIED

THE LOST ONES WHO JEERED

AS I LEFT.

FORMER OCCULT CODES

I CURSED THE ATTACKERS

WITH MY LEVEL BEST

AND FOR THOSE

WHO'VE KNOWN

ME AS A PARTIAL PAGAN,

DON'T CROSS ME.

EVERYTHING YOU DO WILL

RETURN TO YOUR HEAD

AND CONTAMINATE

YOUR SEED. I WILL

NOT LIVE TO SEE IT.

WHAT IS WORSE IS MY FATHER

HAS CURSED YOU AND HE

IS MORE POWERFUL

THAN I.

NAN'S SHADOW SIDE

LITTLE LONDON NAN

GOT DRUNK HERE

ON COCO MARTINIS

AS SHE PLAYED

HER NORMAL CON-GAME

WITH ME.

IT'S TOO BAD

SHE TOSSED ME.

WHO CARES IF SHE LOST ME?

SHE'LL NEVER FOOL ME AGAIN.

8:15 DEPARTURE

I WAS TOLD TO WAIT IN THE BAR

FOR A HALF-BAKED STAR,

BUT I SAID SCREW THAT

AND PUT ON MY WOOL HAT.

I'VE SEEN MANY COME

AND I'VE SEEN MANY GO.

THIS ONE'S A TRUE BUM

AS WE ALL WELL KNOW.

SAWGRASS VISION

ON THE STREET

WHERE MY MOTHER

ONCE SLEPT

YOU LIVED ALONE

IN A GATED COMMUNITY.

SAFE AND SOUND,

LOCKED INSIDE

WHO KNEW

AN INTRUDER

WOULD WALK IN

AND END YOUR LIFE

UNMERCIFULLY.

THE GAME

I AM HERE.

YOU ARE THERE.

IT'S TOO BAD

YOU DIDN'T CLEAR THE AIR.

I WOULD HAVE BEEN

A GOOD FRIEND

WHO DIDN'T USE

YOU, FOR ONE.

INSTEAD, YOU USED ME.

SET A PROUD EXAMPLE…

FOR YOUR MOTHER, SON.

CHASING ME

THE FREAK

TURNED

THE CORNER

AND TRIED TO

JUMP ME

BEFORE

I ENTERED THE PARKING LOT.

DON'T SCREW

WITH ME, PUNK.

I CAN READ DANGER A MILE AWAY…

UNLESS I'M IN LOVE WITH YOU.

NEXT STOP, LOVE

I WILL KNOW YOU

WHEN YOUR HAND

TOUCHES MINE.

THE LAST LAUGH

ON THE NET

YOU THREATEN

THE INNOCENT.

THE ONE LAUGHING IS YOU.

THE ONE WITH THE PEN

IS ME.

IF YOU SILENCE ME,

ANOTHER WILL RISE

TO TELL MY STORY.

TEA POT

A LADY FIRST

SHOWED ME

A ROOM AT THE INN.

I BROUGHT BACK

A TEA POT FOR HER.

I WAS MERELY BEING KIND,

PAYING HER FOR KINDNESS,

WHICH SHE EXPRESSED FIRST.

THE POT MATCHED

HER BED SPREAD

AND SHE LAUGHED

AT THE WEDDED

BLISS OF THE TWO.

IT MADE ME HAPPY

TO BESTOW A GIFT.

I WISHED IT WOULD

HAVE LASTED.

THE ONLY PHYSICIAN

UNDO PAIN

HAS BEEN SUFFERED.

I DO NOT KNOW WHY I

MUST PONDER

THE BEST ROUTE TO

SELF-AWARENESS,

HEALING EVERY PART BROKEN

BEYOND RECOGNITION

OF MY FORMER SELF.

MY LITTLE FRIEND

I THINK SO HIGHLY OF YOU AND I
KNOW YOU'VE BEEN HURT
BY THOSE YOU HAVE TRUSTED.
THE MORNING IS HERE.
THE DAY IS BRIGHT AND CLEAR.
VENTURE OUT OF THE HOUSE
TO SEE WHO YOU CAN FIND.

CLOSED

LOST AND UNMOVED,
THEY MOVE QUICKLY
AWAY FROM THE TOUCH
OF THEIR DAWN.
AWAKEN FROM SLEEP
AND MEET THE SUN.
POUR ITS RADIANCE
OVER STIFF BODIES.
FIND JOY AND PEACE
TO PROPEL YOU FURTHER
INTO YOUR WAKING DREAM.
KNOW ALL CAN BE YOURS.

ANNLILITA

HE SPEAKS OF ANN

AND THE LOVE POURS

FROM EACH

SYLLABLE AND LETTER.

ETERNITY CEASES

AS HE FINDS THE RIGHT DESCRIPTIVE

TO IMPART

THE INNER AND OUTER

BEAUTY OF HER BEING.

LOVE SENT

I KNOW MY HEART
FILLED WITH YOU
AND I SENT YOU LOVE…
UNFULFILLED AND
NO REPLY.
I AM FINISHED
WITH FIGHTING
THE HEART.

THE CAPTIVE

I SEE YOU IN DREAMS AND IN THE YARD.

YOUR EYES SEARCH MINE,

BUT THEY ARE COLD, BEADY, AND BLACK.

I RETURN TO WASHING DISHES,

WRITING POETRY,

MAKING BEDS.

ONCE

YOU LOOKED AT ME

WITH AFFECTION.

BRITTLE AND BROKEN

SPARROW'S FEATHERS

HAVE BEEN PULLED FROM ME IN FLIGHT.

I'VE NOT DIED. I'VE NOT DIED.

MOCK ME THEN,

AS I CONTINUE TO FIGHT.

THE APOSTLE

I DIE EVERY DAY,

REMOVING BRIARS

AND THORNS

FROM CLOTHES

AND EARTHLY FLESH.

GW

GEORGE WASHINGTON

ETCHED HIS INITIALS IN GLASS PANES

BETWEEN BATTLES.

SO, TOO, WE

FOLLOW OUR GENERAL

IN PRAYER.

SPRING NIGHT

TONIGHT

I FORGOT THE WRITER

AS I STOOD

OUTSIDE TO FEEL

THE WARM DECLINE

OF THE DAY

AND LOOK UP INTO THE FACE OF THE

NIGHT.

JOAN NOËLDECHEN HAS BEEN PUBLISHED IN JUNE COTNER'S DOG BLESSINGS, POCKET PRAYERS, HOUSE BLESSINGS, BEDSIDE PRAYERS, AND BLESS THE DAY, IN WHO'S WHO IN AMERICA, WHO'S WHO AMONG AMERICAN WOMEN, BEYOND KATRINA, AND IN VARIOUS JOURNALS AND MAGAZINES. JOAN FOCUSES ON POETRY, WOMEN'S MAINSTREAM FICTION, SCREENWRITING, EDITING, PHOTOGRAPHY, AND MARKETING. HTTP://WWW.MYSPACE.COM/WRITINGSPACES.

POETRY

1997 BEDSIDE PRAYERS (ED. BY JUNE COTNER, HARPERCOLLINS SAN FRANCISCO)

1998 BLESS THE DAY (ED. BY JUNE COTNER, KODANSHA INTERNATIONAL)

2000 ASHES & EMBERS: COMPLETE POEMS 1979-1999 (IUNIVERSE, 2000)

2001 SWING HANGING FROM EVERY TREE (ED. BY SUSAN STONE REYNOLDS, WOOD'N'BARNES PUBLISHING)

2004 HOUSE BLESSINGS (ED. BY JUNE COTNER, COTNER INK)

2005 2006 EVERYDAY BLESSINGS: 365 DAYS OF INSPIRATION, COMFORT, AND GRATITUDE (ED. BY JUNE COTNER, SOURCEBOOKS, INC.)

2005 BEYOND KATRINA (ED. PATRICIA ELLYN POWELL, ARTS & HEALTHCARE PRESS, ARTS COUNCIL OF CENTRAL LOUISIANA)

2006 POCKET PRAYERS (ED. BY JUNE COTNER, CHRONICLE BOOKS)

2006 FOREVER IN LOVE: A CELEBRATION OF LOVE & ROMANCE (ED. BY JUNE COTNER, ANDREWS MCNEEL PUBLISHING)

2007 Miracles of Motherhood: Prayers & Poems for a New Mother (ed. by June Cotner, Center Street/Time Warner Book Group)

2007 To Have & To Hold: Blessings for Newlyweds (ed. by June Cotner, Center Street/Time Warner Book Group)

2008 Dog Blessings (ed. by June Cotner, New World Library)

2008 Takoma Poems (Lulu.com)

2008 To Dream of Dancing (Lulu.com)

2009 Martin Luther King, Jr. – An Anthology of Multicultural Poetry (Western Illinois University)

2009 Serenity Prayers (ed. By June Cotner, Andre McNeal Publishing)

2009 & 2011 The Vortex (Lulu.com)

2011 Betrayal in your beekman arms (Lulu.com)

SCREENPLAYS

2003 Takoma Blue

2004 Borrowed Starling

2007 Dead Actors

2008 London Psychics

2008 Dead Psychics

SCREENPLAYS

with Silvi M. Richardson

1995 And the Angels Sing

1996 Shadowdance

1996 Pasaquan Daze

PLAYS

with Silvi M. Richardson

1996 And the Angels Sing

SHORT STORIES

2011 Dolphin Castle & Other True Tales (Lulu.com)

NOVELS

2000 Dreamers Out of Step (Xlibris)

NOVELLAS

2001 Eve's Song (Great Unpublished)

Journals & Magazines

The Thomas Wolfe Review Spring 1996, Vol. 20, 1

The Angle Street Review, 2000, Vol. II.I

The Oxford American

www.ingramcontent.com/pod-product-compliance
Ingram Content Group UK Ltd.
Pitfield, Milton Keynes, MK11 3LW, UK
UKHW041904190726
13854UKWH00003B/1079

9 781257 567881